Pancho Villa

A Proud Heritage The Hispanic Library

Pancho Villa

Mexican Revolutionary Hero

R. Conrad Stein

The Child's World

Published in the United States of America by The Child's World®
PO Box 326 • Chanhassen, MN 55317-0326 • 800-599-READ • www.childsworld.com

Acknowledgments
The Childs World®: Mary Berendes, Publishing Director
Editorial Directions, Inc.: E. Russell Primm, Editorial Director; Pam Rosenberg, Project Editor;
Melissa McDaniel, Line Editor; Katie Marsico, Assistant Editor; Matt Messbarger, Editorial
Assistant; Susan Hindman, Copyeditor; Susan Ashley and Sarah E. De Capua, Proofreaders;
Chris Simms and Olivia Nellums, Fact Checkers; Timothy Griffin/IndexServ, Indexer; Cian
Loughlin O'Day and Dawn Friedman, Photo Researchers; Linda S. Koutris, Photo Selector
Creative Spark: Mary Francis and Rob Court, Design and Page Production
Cartography by XNR Productions, Inc.

Photos
Cover: Pancho Villa poses for photograph
Cover photograph: Bettmann/Corbis
Interior photographs: Bettmann/Corbis: 8, 9, 10, 11, 13, 19, 24, 30, 31; Corbis: 7 (William
Henry Jackson), 20, 21 (David Muench), 26, 29 (Oscar White), 33 (Daniel Lainé), 34
(Hulton-Deutsch Collection); Getty Images/Hulton|Archive: 14, 15, 18, 28; The Granger
Collection, New York: 17, 23, 25, 27; North Wind Picture Archives: 35.

Library of Congress Cataloging-in-Publication Data
Cataloging-in-Publication data for this title has been applied for and is available from the
United States Library of Congress.

Chapter One

The Legend and the Man

Legends and stories grow around the lives of national heroes. Pancho Villa is a hero in Mexican history. A story that has often been told about Villa supposedly happened when he was 16 years old. One afternoon, the young Villa found his mother standing outside their house shouting at a well-dressed man. The man owned the land where the Villa family farmed. Pancho Villa discovered the reason behind the uproar: The landowner had attacked Pancho's teenage sister. Pancho became furious. He grabbed a pistol and shot the landowner in the foot.

After shooting the rich man, Pancho Villa ran into the hills. There he joined a band of outlaws. The band stole cattle from ranches and robbed trains and banks. Villa learned to shoot and to kill. In the years to come, he was never seen without a gun. Being a

People work at a silver mine in Zacatecas, Mexico, during the late 1800s. In addition to being known for its silver mines, Zacatecas was also the site of several important battles during the Mexican Revolution, including a 1914 conflict involving Pancho Villa.

bandit was a cruel way to live, but it prepared Villa to become a courageous military leader.

Pancho Villa was born on June 5, 1878, in northern Mexico. He was from the state of Durango, a rugged and mountainous region where there is not enough rainfall to support profitable farms. In Villa's time, people held jobs on cattle ranches or worked in silver and tin mines. Mexico was a land of stark contrast between rich and poor. Rich people owned the ranches and the mines. Workers were paid so little that they could barely feed their families.

Villa's family was very poor. He never went to school. When he was seven years old, his father died. The young boy had to help support his four brothers and sisters. He began working at various jobs in mines and on ranches. His favorite job was helping on wagons that carried goods to town. Riding the wagons enabled him to visit many villages in northern Mexico. The wagons also helped develop his lifelong love for horses. It is no wonder Villa later gained fame as a **cavalry** commander, a leader of soldiers on horseback.

Villa's life changed forever when he became a bandit. In Mexico, the word bandit has a different meaning from the word thief. A thief is a dishonest person who

Villa saw firsthand how poverty affected his family and the Mexican people. During the late 1800s, the government was made up of wealthy landowners who gave little thought to the problems faced by the poor.

Many historians doubt the story that Pancho Villa was forced to become a bandit after he defended his sister. The historians say the story is simply a tall tale told about a famous man. But Pancho Villa insisted that the clash between the landowner and his family really occurred.

In 1914, Villa told the story of his life to a writer named Manuel Alcalde. Many years later, Villa's life story was published in a book called *Memorias de Pancho Villa* (Memoirs of Pancho Villa). Villa had told Alcalde, "The tragedy of my life begins on September 22, 1894, when I was sixteen years old." He recalled how he saw his mother screaming at the landowner: "Go away from my house! Why do you want to take my daughter?" According to Villa, he then shot the landowner, fled to the countryside, and became an outlaw. Villa said, "My **conscience** told me I had done the right thing."

steals from friends and neighbors. A bandit, on the other hand, has a touch of Robin Hood in him. Robin Hood was the English folk hero who stole from the rich and gave to the poor. The proper Mexican bandit, or *bandido* in Spanish, was supposed to steal only from the rich. The bandido was also expected to give food and money to poor people.

Was Villa a true bandit? Certainly he gave money to the poor. He once gave hundreds of pesos to an elderly blind man to help him set up a tailor shop. Villa often presented stolen cattle to poor families so that they would have meat. Villa made sure everyone knew about these generous acts. During the Mexican Revolution, newspaper reporters followed Villa's army. When Villa was giving out food to poor villagers, he made certain reporters were present to record the event. Like Robin Hood of old, Villa stole from the rich. However, he also killed rich people when he thought it

According to legend, Robin Hood lived during the 1100s. Historians continue to debate whether the generous outlaw actually existed or was simply the subject of an early English myth.

When Pancho Villa was born, he was given the name Doroteo Arango. When he became a bandit, he changed his name to Pancho Villa, which is pronounced PAHN-cho VEE-ya. He took the name to honor his father's father, whose name was Jesus Villa.

was necessary. He was capable of killing anyone who angered him for the slightest reason.

Friends claimed Villa loved to sing and dance. A muscular man, Villa had a deep laugh that could be heard across a dance floor. But this fun-loving outer face masked a dark and even terrifying inner nature. When Villa was angry, his glare alone could freeze an enemy with fear. Villa could look a man straight in the eyes and shoot him to death without blinking. He would show no mercy. There is a legend that he once forced a man to dig his own grave before killing him.

The Revolution Begins

By the time Pancho Villa was born, Mexico had long been in turmoil. Mexico had once been the home of several large, complex Native American nations, including the Aztecs. In 1521, a Spanish army conquered the mighty Aztecs. For the next 300 years, Spain ruled Mexico. Spain brought the Catholic religion and the Spanish language to Mexico. Mexicans fought a war of independence in 1821 and won their freedom from Spain.

Independence did not bring peace. Instead, Mexico suffered through a series of wars. Mexico fought and lost a disastrous war with the United States from 1846 to 1848. French troops invaded Mexico in 1863 and controlled the country for three years. **Civil wars** rocked Mexico in the 1870s. Finally, an army general named Porfirio Díaz became president in 1876, two years before Pancho Villa's birth.

Conquistador Hernando Cortés and his army conquered the Aztecs in 1521. The natives found themselves powerless against the Spaniards' horses, armor, and guns.

Díaz was determined to make Mexico a modern country. For a model, he looked north to the United States. In the 1870s, the United States built railroads, factories, mines, and thriving farms. Díaz vowed to bring this sort of industry to Mexico. During his time in office, some 9,000 miles (14,484 kilometers) of railroads were constructed and the output of the country's mines tripled. But wages for mine workers and railroad laborers were pitifully low. Díaz refused to spend money to create a modern school system. As a result, only 25 percent of the Mexican people could read or write.

Díaz served as president for nearly 35 years. He claimed he was voted into office in regular elections. In truth, the elections were rigged so that Díaz would always win. The president tolerated no opposition. Rival politicians who sought power were either shot, jailed, or forced to flee the country. Workers who rebelled against their bosses were also treated brutally.

A train crosses a bridge in Mexico during the late 1800s. Porfirio Díaz worked hard to modernize Mexico, but he also made decisions that often had a negative impact on the poor.

In 1908, Francisco Madero, a wealthy landowner, decided to run for president. Madero was thin, bald, and looked more like a schoolteacher than a politician. At first, Díaz ignored Madero because he believed few Mexicans would vote for this mild-mannered gentleman. But by 1910, thousands of people were attending Madero's speeches. Díaz then acted in his usual manner—he had Madero thrown in jail. Madero stayed in jail until after the presidential election of 1910, which Díaz won easily.

While in office, Díaz was sympathetic to the interests of wealthy plantation owners. These men were anxious to acquire more land, and Díaz helped them do it—even when it meant stealing land from poor villagers.

After Francisco Madero was released from jail, he fled to the United States. He then issued a statement that he named after San Luis Potosí, the last city he had stayed in, in northern Mexico. This statement, the

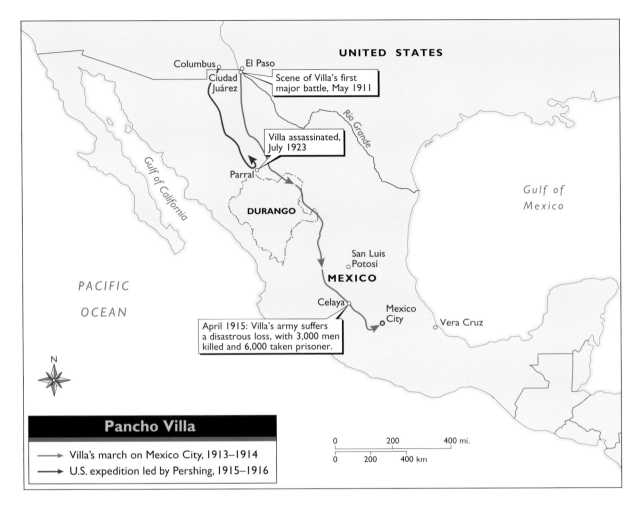

UNITED STATES

Columbus
El Paso
Ciudad Juárez
Scene of Villa's first major battle, May 1911
Río Grande
Villa assassinated, July 1923
Parral
DURANGO
Gulf of California
Gulf of Mexico
San Luis Potosí
MEXICO
PACIFIC OCEAN
Celaya
Mexico City
Vera Cruz
April 1915: Villa's army suffers a disastrous loss, with 3,000 men killed and 6,000 taken prisoner.
N

Pancho Villa

→ Villa's march on Mexico City, 1913–1914
→ U.S. expedition led by Pershing, 1915–1916

0   200   400 mi.
0   200   400 km

Pancho Villa led the people of northern Mexico during the bloody revolution that began in 1910.

Plan of San Luis Potosí, included a startling request. Madero, the peace-loving gentleman, called on the Mexican people to rise up and overthrow the Díaz government by force. Soon, the bloody Mexican Revolution would begin.

It would seem that the bandit Pancho Villa would have little interest in Mexican presidential politics.

But Villa was no ordinary cattle thief. He once told an American writer, "In my [youth] I saw . . . people who were being **oppressed.** [They] had to suffer for the few who became rich. . . . I solemnly swore that I would attack that system and punish it severely."

In November 1910, Villa met with Francisco Madero. It was a strange meeting. Madero was an **idealist;** Villa was a bandit. Yet the two men discussed how to make Mexico a modern and **democratic** country. Villa believed that Madero could help poor people improve their lives. Madero thought a revolution would soon start, and he needed Villa to lead an army.

The Mexican Revolution was never controlled by a single leader. Instead, it was a nationwide uprising of desperate people who were tired of being

Francisco Madero was born into one of the wealthiest families in Mexico. As a politician, however, he showed great concern for Mexico's poor and the challenges they faced under the leadership of Porfirio Díaz.

Pancho Villa and Emiliano Zapata led armies of peasants during the Mexican Revolution. When Díaz failed to listen to the peaceful protests of his people, the poor were forced to take up arms to win back their rights.

ruled by a cruel dictator. At first, two rebel commanders led the revolt. Farmers in the south rallied behind one of their own, a poor farmer named Emiliano Zapata. In the north, miners and ranch hands joined the army of Pancho Villa. Both Zapata and Villa aimed at overthrowing the government of President Díaz. Villa hoped to replace Díaz with Francisco Madero. Zapata did not trust Madero, but he fought to rid Mexico of Díaz.

Villa's first major battle took place in May 1911 in the town of Ciudad Juárez. None of Villa's soldiers had uniforms. Their rifles were old and unreliable. One of their cannons was 70 years old. Camped in Ciudad Juárez was Díaz's army of well-equipped troops. Ignoring the strength of his enemy, Villa attacked the city. Streets exploded into wild gun battles. In the uproar, Villa's men broke into houses and then chopped down walls to enter the houses

Despite their lack of good equipment, the revolutionaries at Ciudad Juárez defeated 700 government soldiers over the course of a few days.

Villa's soldiers occupy the streets of Ciudad Juárez shortly after the fall of the Mexican government. At the time of the Mexican Revolution, Ciudad Juárez was home to about 20,000 people.

next door. In this way, the rebels advanced house to house without exposing themselves to gunfire on the streets. On May 10, the commander of Díaz's army gave up. Pancho Villa had won an astonishing victory.

The fall of Ciudad Juárez gave Villa a gateway to the United States. In the United States, he sold stolen cattle and purchased modern guns for his troops. Villa's victory at Ciudad Juárez also triggered other uprisings throughout Mexico. As warfare raged, 81-year-old Porfirio Díaz left office and sailed to Europe. In June 1911, Francisco Madero entered Mexico City in triumph. Crowds gathered around his carriage shouting, "Viva Madero!" or "Long live Madero!" Mexico held its first honest election in years, and Madero received 90 percent of the vote. With Madero in office, it was thought the revolution would end. Instead, the Mexican Revolution was about to enter a new and very bloody chapter.

Spectators to the Battle

The town of Ciudad Juárez lies across the Rio Grande River (right) from El Paso, Texas. During the battle, residents of El Paso sat on their rooftops and watched the fighting on the other side of the river. Some made bets on which side would win. A few El Paso citizens were wounded by gunshots.

Chapter Three

Mexico at War with Itself

President Francisco Madero vowed to make Mexico
truly democratic. But the country remained in the grip
of hatred and fear. Zapata continued his war against
large landowners. Zapata's battle cry, which later
became the battle cry of the revolution, was "Land
and liberty!" Villa tried to keep his men peaceful in
order to give Madero a chance to be a successful president. But always the bandit, Villa still raided ranches.

A powerful general named Victoriano Huerta
resented Villa for many reasons. Huerta accused
Villa of planning an uprising. Villa turned himself
in to Huerta, knowing he had done nothing wrong.
But General Huerta ordered him shot by a firing
squad. At the last minute, another officer persuaded
Huerta to spare Villa's life. Afterward, Madero kept
Villa in prison.

Villa used his time behind bars to improve his reading. His favorite books were about Napoleon, a famous French general. He also read *The Three Musketeers,* a classic adventure set in France. Eventually, Villa escaped from jail by disguising himself as a lawyer and walking out while holding a handkerchief over his face.

In February 1913, war broke out on the streets of Mexico City. Armies loyal to President Madero fought forces

Victoriano Huerta is remembered as a harsh and cruel dictator who often imprisoned or killed those who opposed him.

commanded by General Huerta. For 10 days, battles swept the crowded city. Far more **civilians** than soldiers were killed. Madero was captured, and on February 22, 1913, one of Huerta's army officers shot and killed Madero.

Venustiano Carranza was elected president of Mexico in 1917. He was assassinated three years later.

The **assassination** of President Madero enraged Pancho Villa. He gathered an army in northern Mexico and promised to crush Huerta. By this time, all of Mexico was aflame with war. Other rebel leaders such as Venustiano Carranza and Alvaro Obregón formed armies and went on the warpath. The American government viewed the fighting in Mexico with alarm. In 1914, President Woodrow Wilson seized the Mexican port of Vera Cruz in an attempt to force Huerta from power and to keep that city from being used for arms shipments. In July 1914, General Huerta quietly slipped out of Mexico City. He was arrested in the United States in 1915, and died in prison early the next year.

Still, warfare consumed Mexico. General fought general. Brother fought brother. The Mexican philosopher Octavio Paz called the revolution a **"fiesta of bullets."** The reasons and causes for the fighting were lost on most people. A character in *The Underdogs,* a novel about the Mexican Revolution, says, "What I can't get into my head is why we go on fighting. Didn't we finish off this man Huerta?"

The American public followed the revolution in newspapers almost as if it were a sporting event. The war below the border had heroes and villains. To many Americans, its greatest hero was Pancho Villa. Americans looked upon cavalry charges as daring feats that recalled the time of knights in shining armor. No cavalry commander in Mexico

In addition to being a famous philosopher, Octavio Paz was also an accomplished author and a foreign ambassador.

was bolder or braver than Pancho Villa. Movies of the time showed Villa riding triumphantly in front of his cavalry. His top fighters were called the dorados, the "golden ones," after their wide-brimmed straw hats. Villa began the revolution leading a gang of about 20 bandits. By 1914, he commanded an army of 50,000 horsemen.

Villa stands next to a poster of himself. As he gained fame in America, photographers, journalists, and filmmakers crossed the border to catch a glimpse of the general in battle.

Pancho Villa's courage in battle was legendary. He always rode at the head of his cavalry. When charging an enemy, his face showed no hint of fear—it was a mask of pure fury. During one of the bloodiest battles of the revolution, Villa's bravery cost the lives of thousands of his followers.

On April 6, 1915, Villa led 30,000 men to the town of Celaya in central Mexico. Villa's foe was General Alvaro Obregón (above). Aggressive as usual, Villa ordered his cavalry soldiers to charge Obregón's positions outside of the town. Dust rose under horse hooves, guns crackled in the air, and the men shouted, "Viva Villa!"

At first, it seemed that Pancho Villa's bold leadership would win yet another battle. But Obregón was a brilliant student of warfare. He had read reports of World War I battles being fought in Europe. Obregón had his men dig trenches and string barbed wire in front of them. Crouching in the cover of the trenches, the men fired at Villa's cavalry with rifles and machine guns. The result was disastrous for the charging soldiers. At Celaya, 3,000 of Villa's men were killed and 6,000 were taken prisoner. Villa's once powerful army never recovered from this blow.

American reporters portrayed Villa as a true Robin Hood, a bandit with a generous heart. John Reed was a popular American news writer who traveled with Villa's army. Reed told American readers how Pancho Villa, the powerful general, sat on the dirt with his men to eat a simple meal of **tortillas** and beans. Reed also reported how Villa fought alongside his men. He wrote, "When the fighting is fiercest, when a ragged mob of fierce brown men with hand bombs and rifles rush the bullet-swept streets of an ambushed town—Pancho Villa is among them like any common soldier."

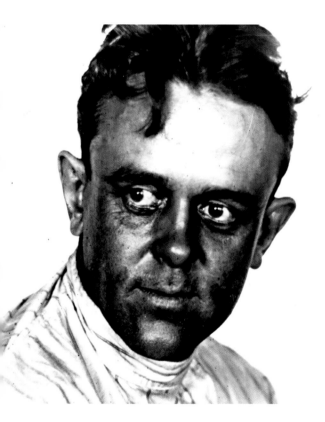

John Reed's articles about Pancho Villa made him famous as a journalist. After covering the Mexican Revolution, Reed traveled to Europe to report on revolutionary politics in countries such as Russia.

Villa, in turn, claimed he liked Americans. But Villa had no love for the American president, Woodrow Wilson. By 1916, the war in Mexico had reached a stage in which generals were battling one another to take control of Mexico. In an effort to bring order there, Wilson backed General Venustiano Carranza. Villa and Carranza were bitter enemies. Villa vowed revenge on the American president.

In the early morning darkness of March 9, 1916, Villa led 485 men across the U.S. border to the town of Columbus, New Mexico. Shouting, "Viva Villa!" and "Viva Mexico!" the horsemen stormed the town's main street. They shot Americans, stole from stores, and set fires. The raid lasted a little more than two hours. When it was over, 17 Americans lay dead and many more were wounded. Most of the victims were innocent civilians.

Since Villa was famous in both America and Mexico, the general expected Woodrow Wilson to support his efforts to become president. Despite the fact that many considered Villa to be the "George Washington of Mexico," Wilson distrusted him and chose to support Venustiano Carranza instead.

The American people exploded in anger over the attack on the town of Columbus. For the first time in more than 100 years, a foreign army had invaded American soil. Pancho Villa was no longer Robin Hood in American eyes—he had turned into a vicious murderer.

President Wilson sent more than 7,000 cavalrymen into Mexico to capture Villa, "dead or alive." The cavalry unit was led by General John Pershing, America's most experienced commander. For 10 months, Pershing probed the mountains of northern

When American troops arrived in Mexico in 1916, they faced several challenges. Although they had better weapons and equipment than Villa, they were unprepared for the extreme heat and the angry villagers who were loyal to the general.

Even though John J. Pershing (above, second from right) never succeeded in capturing Pancho Villa, Woodrow Wilson was impressed by the way Pershing handled himself in a foreign country. Wilson later appointed Pershing to an important military post during World War I.

Mexico. But this was Villa's home ground. He knew every hill and every twist of the road. The Americans tried using airplanes—the first time aircraft ever flew over this region—to hunt down Villa. A reward of $50,000 was posted for information about Villa's hiding place. When told there was such a huge price on his head, Villa joked, "So many pesos for so little a head." But nothing helped. Pershing and his men never found Pancho Villa.

Chapter Four

Death of a Hero

For 10 years, warfare swept Mexico like a fire raging out of control. But even a powerful fire requires fuel to burn. The Mexican Revolution ended in 1920 largely because the people were too exhausted to fight anymore. A government headed by General Alvaro Obregón provided some stability to the war-weary nation.

As a reward for his services during the revolution, Pancho Villa was given a 163,000-acre (65,963-hectare) ranch where he and a select group of his soldiers lived. The ranch lay in the state of Durango, not far from where Villa had been born into a family of poor, landless farmers. On his ranch, Villa lived a life of **luxury**—perhaps too much luxury. Critics claimed Villa became as greedy as the rich landowners he had once fought against. He hired a group of thugs to drive away

Horses roam the rugged landscape in Durango, Mexico. When Villa retired to a ranch there, he employed 50 guards to protect him from the many enemies he had made over the years.

desperately poor farmers who lived on some of his lands. His taste in friends changed. He began to enjoy the company of his fellow landowners.

On July 20, 1923, Villa drove an open car through the town of Parral in northern Mexico. On a street corner, a man who was selling candy from a pushcart saluted and shouted the old war cry, "Viva Villa!" Villa slowed down the car to return the salute. Suddenly, shots fired by hidden gunmen rang out. Villa was hit by

Pancho Villa is still regarded as a hero by some and a villain by others. Despite these conflicting views, he will always be remembered for his military leadership and the role he played in the Mexican Revolution.

nine bullets. He died instantly. It is believed that government agents were behind the attack. Many powerful people in government circles feared Villa would someday try to become president.

After his death, Villa's image as a hero grew even stronger in the hearts of Mexicans. Songs and poems were written in his honor. For years after he died, poor families prayed to Villa as if he were a Catholic saint. Why was this man, who killed others with ease, so beloved in Mexico? First, he was a fearless fighter in war. He fought for the cause of Mexico's poorest people. He also baffled the armies of the United States. Many Mexicans looked upon their powerful neighbor to the north as a bully. Villa outfoxed this bully and won cheers in the process.

Pancho Villa was a complex man who lived in violent times. Perhaps his place in Mexican history can best be seen in the lines of a song popular during his time. In this song, a soldier asks a dove to spread the message of Pancho Villa:

The rich with all their money
Have already got their lashing. . .
Fly, fly away, little dove
And say that Villa has come
To drive [the rich] out forever.

Counting Lives Lost

Most Americans believe that the U.S. Civil War, which lasted from 1861 to 1865, was the bloodiest war ever fought on the North American continent. This belief is false. More than 500,000 Americans lost their lives during the Civil War. No one knows exactly how many people died during the Mexican Revolution of 1910 to 1920. But most historians estimate that at least 1 million and perhaps as many as 2 million Mexicans died as a direct result of the war.

1521–1821: Spain rules over Mexico.

1876: General Porfirio Díaz becomes president of Mexico.

1878: Pancho Villa is born Doroteo Arango in the state of Durango in northern Mexico on June 5.

1885: Pancho Villa's father dies.

1894: According to legend, 16-year-old Villa shoots a wealthy landowner who had attacked his sister. Villa flees his home and becomes an outlaw.

1908: Francisco Madero announces he will run for president. Díaz later has Madero thrown in jail.

1910: Madero issues the Plan of San Luis Potosí, which calls for the people to rise up and overthrow Díaz. The Mexican Revolution begins. Francisco Madero and Pancho Villa meet to discuss the future of Mexico.

1911: Villa captures the border city of Ciudad Juárez after a violent battle. Díaz resigns as president of Mexico. Madero is elected president in October.

1912: Villa is accused of planning an uprising and narrowly escapes facing a firing squad. He is later sentenced to jail.

1913: Madero is assassinated by an army officer under the command of General Victoriano Huerta.

1914: American soldiers occupy the port city of Vera Cruz in April. Huerta flees Mexico City in July.

1915: Villa counts on American support to obtain the Mexican presidency. Instead the U.S. government supports Venustiano Carranza. Villa's forces fight a bloody battle against an army commanded by General Alvaro Obregón.

1916: Villa leads a group of soldiers on a raid into the town of Columbus, New Mexico, and kills 17 Americans.

1916–1917: American cavalry units commanded by General John Pershing spend 10 months searching northern Mexico for Pancho Villa, but do not find him.

1920: The Mexican Revolution ends. The bloody revolution has claimed the lives of at least 1 million and perhaps as many as 2 million Mexicans.

1923: Pancho Villa is assassinated on July 20.

assassination (uh-SASS-suh-nay-shuhn) An assassination is the murder of an important political figure. The assassination of Pancho Villa took place in 1923.

cavalry (KAV-uhl-ree) A cavalry is an army of soldiers on horseback. Pancho Villa commanded a cavalry of 50,000 men.

civilians (si-VIL-yuhnz) Civilians are people who are not members of the armed forces of a country. Many thousands of civilians were killed during the Mexican Revolution.

civil wars (SIV-il WORS) Civil wars are wars that are fought between two different groups within the same country. Civil wars were fought in Mexico during the 1870s.

conscience (KON-shuhnss) A conscience is the ability to tell right from wrong and it makes you feel guilty when you do something that you know is wrong. When Pancho Villa shot his sister's attacker and became a bandit, his conscience told him it was the right thing to do.

democratic (dem-uh-KRAT-ik) A country is democratic if the people freely elect their leaders. Francisco Madero wanted to make Mexico a democratic nation.

fiesta (fee-ESS-tuh) A fiesta is a festival. Writer Octavio Paz called the Mexican Revolution a "fiesta of bullets."

idealist (eye-DEE-uhl-ist) An idealist is someone who has certain high goals and acts to achieve them. Francisco Madero was an idealist.

luxury (LUHG-zhuh-ree) Luxury is the condition of great comfort and wealth. After the Mexican Revolution ended, Pancho Villa lived a life of luxury.

oppressed (uh-PRESST) To be oppressed is to be crushed or held down. Pancho Villa believed that the Mexican people were oppressed by the wealthy.

tortillas (tor-TEE-yuhz) Tortillas are thin, round pieces of bread. Pancho Villa ate tortillas with his men.

Books

Carroll, Bob. *Pancho Villa*. San Diego, Calif.: Lucent Books, 1996.

Marcovitz, Hal. *Pancho Villa*. Philadelphia: Chelsea House, 2003.

O'Brien, Steven. *Pancho Villa*. New York: Chelsea House, 1994.

Stein, R. Conrad. *The Mexican Revolution: 1910–1920*. New York: Macmillan, 1994.

Web Sites

Visit our Web page for lots of links about Pancho Villa:
http://www.childsworld.com/links.html

Note to parents, teachers, and librarians: We routinely check our Web links to make sure they're safe, active sites—so encourage your readers to check them out!

About the Author

R. Conrad Stein was born in Chicago, Illinois. At age 18, he enlisted in the U.S. Marines and served for three years. He later attended the University of Illinois and earned a degree in history. Mr. Stein is a full-time writer. Over the years, he has published more than 150 books, mostly history and geography titles. The author was especially pleased to write for A Proud Heritage because he lived in Mexico for seven years during the 1970s. The Stein family still spends most of the summer months in the town of San Miguel de Allende in central Mexico. The rest of the year, Mr. Stein lives in Chicago with his wife, children's book author Deborah Kent, and their daughter, Janna.